I0140116

Ceremonial Magic

Ceremonial Magic Guide for Beginners

Ceremonial Magic Overview, Basics Rituals, Theories, Macrocosm and Microcosm, History, Healing and Banishing Techniques, Cabala, Psychic Energy, and More!

By Riley Star

Copyrights and Trademarks

All rights reserved. No part of this book may be reproduced or transformed in any form or by any means, graphic, electronic, or mechanical, including photocopying, recording, taping, or by any information storage retrieval system, without the written permission of the author.

This publication is Copyright ©2018 NRB Publishing, an imprint. Nevada. All products, graphics, publications, software and services mentioned and recommended in this publication are protected by trademarks. In such instance, all trademarks & copyright belong to the respective owners. For information consult www.NRBpublishing.com

Disclaimer and Legal Notice

This product is not legal, medical, or accounting advice and should not be interpreted in that manner. You need to do your own due-diligence to determine if the content of this product is right for you. While every attempt has been made to verify the information shared in this publication, neither the author, neither publisher, nor the affiliates assume any responsibility for errors, omissions or contrary interpretation of the subject matter herein. Any perceived slights to any specific person(s) or organization(s) are purely unintentional.

We have no control over the nature, content and availability of the web sites listed in this book. The inclusion of any web site links does not necessarily imply a recommendation or endorse the views expressed within them. We take no responsibility for, and will not be liable for, the websites being temporarily unavailable or being removed from the internet.

The accuracy and completeness of information provided herein and opinions stated herein are not guaranteed or warranted to produce any particular results, and the advice and strategies, contained herein may not be suitable for every individual. Neither the author nor the publisher shall be liable for any loss incurred as a consequence of the use and application, directly or indirectly, of any information presented in this work. This publication is designed to provide information in regard to the subject matter covered.

Neither the author nor the publisher assume any responsibility for any errors or omissions, nor do they represent or warrant that the ideas, information, actions, plans, suggestions contained in this book is in all cases accurate. It is the reader's responsibility to find advice before putting anything written in this book into practice. The information in this book is not intended to serve as legal, medical, or accounting advice.

Foreword

The thing that sets us apart from other creatures in this world is our ability to think. The ability to become aware of the physical world around us makes us not just physical beings but also mental beings. Everything in life is pretty much the result of human thinking. Everything starts with a thought. The good news is that the universe is mental too! This is why there are lots of books out there, particularly in the self – help area that emphasizes about controlling one's thoughts because this is part of how a person can achieve magnificent results in life. As the old cliché goes, everything starts in the mind.

There are many systems that have been developed throughout the ages that teach people on how to control one's thoughts in order to achieve anything in life, one of which is the art of Ceremonial Magic. Occult magic is one of the oldest systems that studies psychic forces by using mental training, a system of symbols, and concentration to connect with the inner self and 'program' the mind. Its main purpose is to alter one's self, and the environment according to one's will.

Most of the concepts of ceremonial magic that still exists today came from the ancient Egyptians. However, other people from the west and the east like the Chinese,

Tibetans, and Hindus have also developed their own system of ceremonial magic based from their own belief and religious systems. Although the art of ceremonial magic was suppressed because of the rise of Christianity back in the day, it was rediscovered during the medieval age in Europe – thanks to the alchemists and Cabalists. And it's not until after about a century when western culture began studying, and practicing this ancient art.

In the turn of the 20th century, science has somewhat shown interest about the ancient system, and sort of categorized it under the field of psychology. Today, through parapsychology (branch of psychology that deals with psychic phenomena), people are gaining insights in how the mind can affect one's environment, and how a person can tap into their 'psychic ability' to create the life he/she truly desire.

This book will provide you with information about the ancient system of ceremonial magic. You'll get an overview of how the system works, why it is important, the different elements and forces, the basic rituals, and everything related to it. Once you learned how to become aware of your subconscious, it'll be easier for you to control your conscious mind and surroundings. Be truly amazed about what the mind can do! Let the magic begin!

Table of Contents

Introduction to Ceremonial Magic

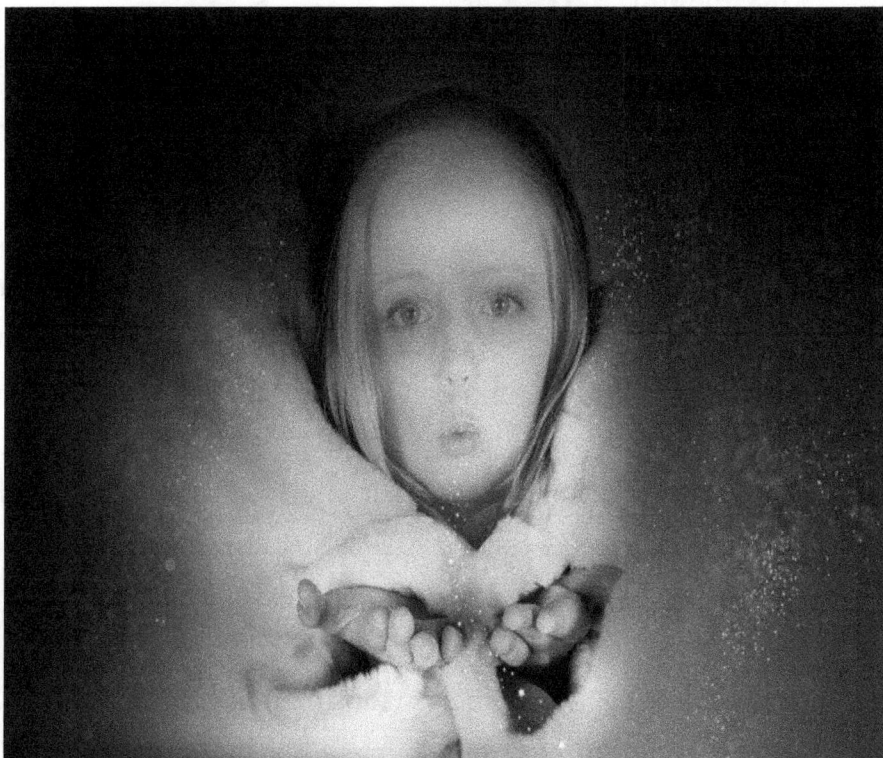

"The universe is a projection of ourselves; an image as unreal as that of our faces in the mirror"

- Aleister Crowley

Magic encompasses many different fields including philosophy, science, psychology, art, religion, and metaphysics. It is something that is always in the borderlines of the 'unknown' so to speak. However, in the field of psychic phenomena, magic can help one understand the universe, and fit the puzzles of life into something meaningful.

A person's awareness of the physical world is mostly based upon the five senses (sight, hearing, smell, touch and taste). These physical senses are in charge of continually sending information to your mind both consciously or subconsciously. After receiving external information, your mind will then interpret it so that the world around you and whatever's happening will make sense because this will help you act accordingly. How a person interprets information will be based from how his/her mind is programmed. This means that one's subconscious will follow a subconscious mental photograph of the person's belief about the world, and what the world looks like (ex: worldview, mindset, belief system). This subconscious mental photograph or program is built up from an individual's personal experiences over time, culture, religious background, upbringing, behavior around people, and/or influences from friends or family. Your thoughts, feelings, attitude, and habits towards certain things are all based upon your subconscious model or mental program.

Now, I know what you're thinking! "If that's the case, then nobody is exactly right about everything? Right?" Yes! Because if you really think about it, we all have different versions of 'truth' since it's based from our own experiences – and no one in this world ever experienced or learned the exact same thing at the exact same manner. We may learn general information but the way our own minds will interpret it or make a conclusion about it is a result of a combination of our other personal experiences that others may not have experienced. This means that everything is subjective. We only see an aspect of every single thing but not the whole picture. So, how can we know the "real truth"?

There's a separate reality that lies within each of us – our inner self. The inner self is something that is often ignored unless a person seeks it. In magic, the inner self is also known as the "true will." This is the center of consciousness and one's identity. This is the 'real you.' And since everything is just based on external conditions which can sometimes produce false information, your true will serves as your inner compass.

One's will is the axiom of (ceremonial) magic. This true will expresses our innermost desires. The problem with life is that most of the time we get what we don't want or we tend to want and get something that is not ultimately good for us because the 'truth' is tricked by our outer illusions.

A concrete example can be if your parents got divorced, and growing up you always see them constantly fighting. Usually, kids of divorced parents ended up being divorced themselves, and do sort of self – sabotage their relationships even if they don't want to (deep inside). Either that or they simply get attracted to the wrong people. This is because their subconscious mind already got tricked, and was used to these kinds of outer conditions, it became familiar, it became normal, no matter how awful it is (divorce, broken family etc.). Such conditions unfortunately, make them feel "safe." Their mind is telling them it feels like "home." And even if they consciously know it's not good for them, their subconscious mind tends to fall back into this trap.

It already formed a belief system in them that "being in a relationship will always end up as a disaster," and to prove this interpretation, it has to manifest outwardly making them naturally attracted to the wrong person or doing self – sabotage in their relationships.

Perhaps the main purpose of studying the art of ceremonial magic is to help a person 'override' their own mental system that they have accumulated over the years. It will require a great amount of determination if you want to change your mental program. You need to unlearn things, create new habits and also sustain it so that permanent change can occur. Magicians or those who apply the art of ceremonial magic are in touch with their true feelings and inner self. The job of a magician is to awaken one's awareness of the true will and teach people to be free of outer conditionings.

Chapter One: Understanding Ceremonial Magic

As mentioned earlier, magic is closely related with psychic energy or psychic forces. And although the exact nature of such forces is quite subtle and still pretty much unknown, there are definitely energies that powers it based on many experiments and studies that had been carried out ever since. One of the reasons why people study and do ceremonial magic even after all these years is because it's beneficial to one's mental and physical health, it is a powerful tool that can alter events so that a person can achieve one's goals and desires, and because it's also fun and very interesting.. It will surely be a learning experience for anyone who will apply it. Let's get started!

Brief History of Ceremonial Magic

The art of magic originated during the time of the ancient Egyptians. Ancient magicians are described as someone who is enclosed in sanctified vestments and is carrying sort of what now known as 'magic wand' inscribed with hieroglyphic symbols. The magician is said to control invisible or non – physical beings like elements and energies in the astral world through the use of certain magic words, rituals and symbols. The antiquity of ceremonial magic is not necessarily evil; it's also not made for evil. In fact one of its primary functions is to make people's lives better through harnessing the universe's energy and controlling one's life. However, evil arose from it because people created false schools of sorcery known today as "black magic."

Egypt became the center of learning during the ancient times. It is where many of the fundamentals of arts and sciences as well as technology began. It propelled ideal surroundings for transcendental experimentation along with scientific discoveries. Unfortunately, this is where black magicians of Atlantis also learned the craft of magic and sorcery, and practice their psychic abilities until they completely learned everything they can about the morals of primitive mysteries in this world. Such 'evil' sorcerers started to systematically destroy important keys to ancient wisdom so that one won't be able to learn the knowledge of magic without being part of their occult group. What they did was mutilated the rituals of primitive mysteries while professing to preserve it; this is a strategic play to prevent neophytes from securing the knowledge to which one is entitled.

Idolatry was eventually introduced to encourage neophytes to become worshippers of images of false gods. Such false representations were given emblems and elaborate philosophies and theologies to create confusion and probably test the minds of their devotees. The masses eventually became slaves of these black magicians and cultivated ignorance among worshippers. Superstition then followed, while black magicians fully dominated national affairs resulting to them suffering from the 'priest crafts' of ancient Egypt.

While all of this is going on, another occult group that formed the medieval Cabalists devoted their lives to learning the art of ceremonial magic because they are convinced that their own scriptures sanctioned it. This is why the Cabala magic or Cabala philosophy is perhaps the original basis of ceremonial magic thereafter. It is founded by the ancient magical formulas of King Solomon which was considered as the 'Prince of Ceremonial Magicians' by the Jewish people during that time.

Parapsychology and Magic

Ceremonial magic is now categorized under the field of psychology particularly parapsychology since it is mostly concerned with psychic forcer or phenomena. It is believed that everyone has some psychic ability, and through ceremonial magic an individual can perhaps unlock or tap into this psychic potential. There are numerous types of psychic phenomena, and it is separated into 2 groups: Extra Sensory Perception, and Psychokinesis. This is essential in understanding the concepts, rituals, and processes of ceremonial magic.

Extra Sensory Perception (ESP)

Extra Sensory Perception is when the mind receives information through paranormal means, and not through the five senses. In theory, it is received from psychic forces that come from the outside of the body. Here are the following examples:

- **Clairvoyance**: Also known as remote viewing, this is the ability to see/sense distant objects, places or people non – physically. People who see spirits or ghosts are usually clairvoyant.

- **Clairaudience:** Also known as remote hearing, quite similar to clairvoyance, this is where one hears paranormal beings or information.

- **Traveling Clairvoyance or Astral Projection**: This is the ability to fully experience being in a remote location while the physical body is sleeping. Much like being in a dream but it feels absolutely real as if you're in it.

- **Psychometry:** This is the ability to read and gain information by just touching physical things.

- **Telepathic Receiver or Telepathy:** Commonly known as mental telepathy, this is the ability to receive a thought or communication from other people at a distance without any physical connection to the sender.

- **Precognition:** the ability to foresee the future

- **Retrocognition:** gaining knowledge from the past through paranormal means.

Psychokinesis (PK)

Psychokinesis is pretty much the opposite of ESP because it pertains to the sending side of the psychic phenomena. In theory, PK is when the psychic force is being sent out from the individual instead of just receiving information. Here are the following examples:

- **Telepathic Sender:** the ability to send out a thought or communication to other people at a distance without any physical connection to the receiver/s.

- **Pyschokinesis:** Also known as telekinesis, this is the ability to move or transfer objects through psychic force. Quite same along the lines of "noisy ghosts" wherein physical objects move or sounds are heard. Usually, it involves the presence of a human which acts as an agent that could be the source of the psychic energy.

- **Psychic Healing:** This is the ability to heal illnesses through using the psychic energy of the healer

- **Teleportation and Levitation:** The ability to float or move to other places without using any source of physical support but rather one's psychic energy.

Systems of Magic

Ceremonial magic always involve self – hypnosis or the ability to hypnotize or 'psyche' oneself. But of course, there's more to magic than that. It will also involve what seem to be objective forces like deities, spiritual beings, and other cosmic forces that have an independent existence. Repetitive physical movements like what's being done during rituals can generate psychokinetic forces, though some people argue that the systems, forces, or rituals that may be involved is subjective to the magician, and that such spirits or gods are only archetypes that the magician uses to energize his own vitality. Most magical effects is produced through self – hypnosis or tapping into one's inner self/ subconscious.

When doing ceremonial magic, complexity is not really necessary even if it's an ancient system of symbolism. Most magicians only follow medieval systems because it is traditional, and quite convenient. It also seems to fit the thought process of modern practitioners. Traditional symbols are also believed to have greater emotional effect since it is more familiar but then it is highly subjective. The important thing is that the model or system that a magician uses is understood and programmed in a way that the cosmological system corresponds. You'll learn more about such systems in the next chapters to come, so just keep reading and open your mind!

Chapter Two: The Basics of Ceremonial Magic

Now that you have an idea about what ceremonial magic is it's time to go deeper into this ancient art and system that had been developed during ancient times. This chapter will cover the basic things about ceremonial magic including the different 'worlds,' occult philosophies, and its types. These things are also essential for you to understand the concepts that are related to ceremonial magic; it will also give you a preview of the basic rituals and 'magic' techniques that will be discussed in the next few chapters. The ancients described human beings as mind, body, and soul. During the 20th century, psychologists added that men are also subconscious beings. Let's discover more about it.

The Four Worlds

Humans are now described as physical, mental (conscious mind), spiritual (soul), and astral (subconscious) beings. And because of this it produces a four – fold classification:

- **Spiritual Beings**: Intuitive Qualities
- **Mental Beings**: Rational Thought
- **Astral Beings**: Emotions/Feelings
- **Physical Beings**: Physical Senses/Body

Therefore, according to parapsychology, the universe can be divided into the following 'worlds':

- **Spiritual World**
- **Mental World**
- **Astral World**
- **Physical World**

Our subconscious or the astral body is what magicians call as the 'psychic link,' it includes a person's intuition, psychic abilities, and magical skills. This psychic links are the things that connect us to the physical world and vice – versa.

The astral world is also known as the realm of visual imagination. According to Brenna, it can be both a state of mind, and place at the same time. This is important because most magical or psychic – related phenomena starts with the invisible, and the non – physical realm. It begins in something without the use of the five senses. However, it is important to note that when it comes to tapping into the inner self or understanding psychic phenomena, one should keep in mind that the four worlds interacts with one another. It is not just about the astral or mental world. Energy flows and starts from the spirit to the mind, then it go to one's astral being before it is manifested in the physical world. This is why the physical world is said to only be a projection of the 'inner worlds' or our other state of beings. These higher worlds (spiritual, mental, astral) is the center of a person's consciousness.

Other terms are used by other occult groups, some of which includes the following:

- Astral world is also known as astral light (which can also refer to a non – physical realm)
- Inner planes/ Invisible world are the other terms of the four worlds.

- Vehicles/Sheats/Vessel are same terms pertaining to bodies
- Astral and Mental are also divided into two parts; the upper part (also known as causal body), and the lower part.

Microcosm and Macrocosm

The terms microcosm and macrocosm are part of traditional occult philosophy used in ceremonial magic. Macrocosm simply refers to the greater universe which includes everything that exists while microcosm refers to the 'tiny universe' like us humans because we are somewhat a mini – replica of the universe or macrocosm. This basic magical relationship is cited in the bible wherein God is the macrocosm, and man is the microcosm which means that humanity and god/universe match each other.

In ceremonial magic, the magician is a microcosm that is highly connected to the macrocosm/universe. And since the universe is reflected within man and vice - versa, there's a relationship of energies that exists between man and everything in the universe. I remember a line from the film Star Wars, "I am one with the Force, the Force is with me." We are indeed "one with the force," this is a very important theory relating to ceremonial magic, astrology, and the inner world.

Types of Magic

The main types of magic are personal magic, active magic, and passive magic.

Personal Magic

This refers to the magic that is use to affect one's self or one's state of mind. In today's world, this is mostly used in psychological treatment like therapies, yoga, meditation, and other similar mental techniques. It usually involves self – hypnosis, positive affirmations, self – suggestion, mind re – programming, and the likes.

Active Magic

Active magic or direct magic as in psychokinesis (PK) is the kind that affects the outer world. It involves affecting someone or something or to bring about an occurrence.

Passive Magic

Passive magic as in extra sensory perception (ESP) is the kind that affects the outside through non – physical cause.

It is believed that each of us possesses such magic or psychic abilities, and only differs in degrees. Some are better at manifesting active magic, while some are more passive. It's very rare for a person to be good at all types but of course, through constant practice and training one can excel or improve in using their psychic potential.

The forces of magic are neutral but according to various systems developed over many centuries, there are good and bad or evil forces that are behind it.

White Magic

Good magic is commonly known as white magic. White magic pertains to using one's energy and the universe's energies for unselfish purposes. It usually involves people who uses such energy to do good like in healing illnesses, and influencing one's mind positively or with permission from the person they're trying to're – programmed.'

Black Magic

Black magic or evil magic refers to the kind that only serves one's self or using the energies for selfish reasons. It involves a person healing or influencing one's mind without their permission. When a person uses his/her psychic abilities to control/force another person's will without asking permission or which of course can be considered as black magic. There are many people or magicians who claims to be 'Satanists,' devil worshippers, or black magicians. They are usually charlatans, hoaxers, and dabblers or usually misinformed. They could be attracted to black magic or by doing something that are against the true purpose of ceremonial magic.

It's important to note that if you do encounter a black magician or someone who actually worships Satan you should do your best to stay away from them because these people may have dedicated their lives to becoming evil.

Other Kinds of Magic

While most of us associate white magic with good deeds and unselfish intents, and black magic with Satan worship, animal/human sacrifice, dangerous magical practices, it's important that's it's all a matter of degree. White magic or self – interest magic can also be called gray magic because it may not actually benefit anyone, it must be constructive magic for it to work.

Other kinds also include aversive magic which is the kind that intends to work against the 'natural order.' There's also the so – called high magic (also known as 'the Great Work') involving spiritual alchemy. There's also low magic which is mostly concerned with the physical world.

Keep in mind that any kind of magic can produce side effects regardless of one's intention or desire. Whether or not you have achieved your purpose, it's important to be aware of the possible results because it can potentially affect not just one's state of being but also that of others.

Ceremonial Magic is a Continuous Process

Like any other things in life, the art of ceremonial magic is a continuous process. Your subconscious mind never rests, your surroundings constantly changes and affects how you think. It's important that you always practice and increase your knowledge especially if you are serious about becoming a proficient magician.

Most people only feel subtle effects of magic or this self – hypnosis techniques but as you deal with the subject more, your awareness of the other worlds, the energy flow of your psychic energy, and how it is related to one another increases. This is when your true will is likely to manifest, your life tends to follow what you truly desire deep down which is why having a positive outlook in life can be very beneficial because it sets gives you a better and more positive mindset.

Tips on How to Better Understand Ceremonial Magic

Create a 'Magical' Record

It's very helpful to write down your progress when it comes to applying the concepts, experiments, and rituals of ceremonial magic. You can also include astrological data or other things related to the art of magic as well as keeping records of your dreams especially the things that you think is quite significant to your life as dreams comes from our subconscious mind, it can tell you a lot about yourself and it can also reveal premonitions.

Use Affirmations

Our minds particularly our subconscious is always open to suggestions. Such suggestions usually come from what our five senses have gathered over the years, and the more we experience such circumstances or do it in repetition, the more it is likely to retain in our subconscious which can affect our overall perception, and can ultimately affect one's physical world. This is why using (positive) affirmations are important because it creates positive suggestions to your psyche. And if you continue to repeat such affirmations to yourself aloud or in your mind, it can change and develop such qualities you want to have within yourself. Make sure to repeat positive affirmations every day or several times a day especially before you sleep at night. Affirmations have subtle effects but it can create long – term changes which can help you become better as a person and a potential magician.

Do Visualizations

Visualizations are also another great way to increase your awareness in your spiritual, mental, and astral being. It is usually used to influence one's subconscious. What you can do is to use a simple banishing technique. Banishing is used in magic to get rid of the negative vibes. All you need to do is to visualize a strong white light that flows at the top of your head and over your whole body, then imagine throwing away the negative vibes, you can use hand gestures as well. Keep this up for about 30 minutes or longer every day. You can also apply this technique whenever you're feeling worried or angry because it's a great way to help you deal with your present emotions.

Chapter Three: Elements and Forces

Based on ancient traditions, there are 4 basic elements or principles; these are earth, fire, air, and water. This viewpoint have changed over years with the advancements of science and philosophy but in ceremonial magic, the four elements are still widely used and accepted because it is believed to be closely linked with human emotions, psyche, and the natural forces compared to the modern explanations developed recently in other similar fields. This chapter will cover the different symbols of energies, the qualities of the elements, the significance of these forces, and its relationship with ceremonial magic especially when performing rituals.

Basics of Elements and Forces

The so – called magical elements (earth, fire, air, water) are also used in the field of astrology. Many occult groups believed that these elements are forces of energy or qualities of the energy around us which is highly linked in our astral beings or emotional world. Each element has its own symbols and color, and these are still used by traditional occultists when performing magic rituals today. Other systems like the Tattvic symbols from the eastern culture uses different colors and symbols but the elements and its significance are quite similar.

Elements/ Forces	Symbol	Color
Earth	Triangle pointing down w/ a horizontal line crossing through the middle	Brown; green
Fire	Triangle pointing upwards	red
Air	Triangle pointing up w/ a horizontal line crossing through the	yellow

	middle	
Water	Triangle pointing downwards	blue

One of magic's importance is that it's a field that sees relationships between things just like in astrology, palmistry, tarot reading, and other similar fields wherein they try to relate phenomena with almost everything in life so that one can better understand why such events are happening or the possible message that the universe is trying to communicate.

This relationship in ceremonial magic is called correspondence. Keep in mind though that magical correspondences or relationships are usually not taken literally or the relationship between 2 objects/ phenomena is not equal to one another but they're somehow related (such as gold equals sun in ceremonial magic). This means that one symbol/ object/ phenomena is merely a suggestion to its related meaning/ correspondence. What magicians should do to vividly affect his/her senses is to surround oneself with many appropriate correspondences so that the connection to the inner worlds is more lucid.

In tarot cards, the correspondences are called the 4 suits which are still the same with the magical elements. The term 4 quarters pertains to the direction of the universe. In other fields, Archangels are used to correspond to the 4 magical elements. Astrology signs or zodiac signs are also equal to these magical elements. See the Correspondence Table below:

Correspondence Table

Magical Elements	Suits	Quarter	Archangel	Astrology
Earth	Pentacles	North	Uriel	Taurus Virgo Capricorn
Fire	Wands	South	Michael	Aries Leo Sagittarius
Air	Swords	East	Raphael	Gemini Libra Aquarius
Water	Cups	West	Gabriel	Cancer Scorpio Pisces

Elementals

Mythological entities or so – called elementals are also related to magical elements, and it is believed that such elementals are peopled by spiritual beings. Such elementals are also grouped into 4 categories. Earth is represented by Gnomes; Fire is represented by Salamander; Air is represented by Sylph; Water is represented by Undine. See the table below:

Gnome (Earth)	Salamander (Fire)	Sylph (Air)	Undine (Water)
Dwarfs	Jin or Genies	Fairies	Nymphs
Elves		Storm Angels	Mermaids
Brownies			Harpies
Leprechauns			Sirens
Hobgoblins			Tritons
			Mermen

Elementals can only be seen by those who possess clairvoyant sight abilities. These creatures or elementals are usually seen at night. It's mostly common being seen in mountains or far – flung places especially if the person is sleepy or tired. These elementals exists naturally in the world whether you can see it or not, or believe in it or not. Based on ancient tradition, it's also possible to create an artificial elemental or one that can only exist for a limited time since elemental beings are immortal.

To the ancient Egyptians, such elementals are the universe's physical explanation but many contemporary and modern occult groups see these elementals only as symbols of magical forces, though some still believe that these creatures are real and do exists with us.

Yin Yang and Magical Elements

In eastern culture, the idea of polarity (opposite pairs) is also related to the magical elements. Chinese philosophy has its own set of symbols and has assigned different things to the 4 elements. Occult groups also suggest that everything in the universe can be similarly arranged into related polarities. Below are example of polarities relating to the magical elements in Chinese philosophy:

Yin	Yang
Water	Fire
Contraction	Expansion
Cold	Hot
Feminine	Masculine
Negative	Positive
Passive	Active
Ebb	Flow
Wane	Wax

Chapter Four: Preparing the Mind and Body: Chakras and Meditation

Based from Indian philosophy, humans possess psychic centers or chakras in the body. There are 7 major chakras that links, connects, bridge or serve as energy transformers of the physical body to higher energies. The major chakras can also change pure energies into various forms and connect it with the 4 worlds (mental, astral, spiritual and physical). This chapter will cover the significance of these chakras when harnessing the energy in the universe, and how it is related to the ceremonial magic philosophy. We'll also discuss chakra meditation, and some techniques used by magicians to tap into their inner strength.

Chakras or Psychic Centers

Chakras can be found along the network of psychic channels or nerves, in Hindu these channels is known as 'nadies.' It is along an individual's autonomic nervous system that's connected in the spinal cord.

Chakras are also related with the so – called governing vessel meridian, which is a term used in acupuncture. In Chinese philosophy, chakras are equal to the acupuncture points of the body. The 7 chakras are linked by 3 nerves or nadies that are parallel and also near one another. The middle nadie is known as *sushumna*, which is known to have neutral characteristics. The left side nadie (found near your left hand) is called *ida nadi* and it has yin (more negative) qualities. The right side nadie (found near your right hand) is called *pingal nadie* and it has yang (more positive) qualities.

Chakras can be mostly seen by people who possess clairvoyant sight abilities. They see it as colored circles or funnels that are rotating around the major chakra points in the body. In Eastern philosophy, chakra circles are also described us flowers/ lotuses. The representation of colors for each chakras can vary from one system to another. Aside from these major chakras, there are also many minor chakras that can be found all over the body.

The 7 Major Chakras

The First Chakra: This is also known as the *root chakra* or *muladhara* in Hindu terms. It can be found at the base of the spine particularly at the perineum part of the body. It mainly relates to the earth element as well as the psychic smell.

The Second Chakra: This is also known as the *sacral center or splenic*. It can be found above and also behind the genital or pelvic area. It mainly relates to the water element as well as the psychic taste.

The Third Chakra: This is also known as the *solar plexus or manipura* in Hindu terms. It can be found at the navel area of the body. It mainly relates to the fire element as well as the psychic sight or the clairvoyance. It also corresponds with one's emotions.

The Fourth Chakra: This is also known as the *heart chakra or anahata* in Hindu terms. It can be found at the chest area in the heart. It mainly relates to the air element as well as the psychic touch.

The Fifth Chakra: This is also known as the *throat chakra or vishuddha* in Hindu terms. It can be found at the thyroid area at the base of the throat. It corresponds with psychic hearing or the clairaudience.

The sixth and seventh chakras are two of the most important chakras because they are mostly related to the elevated states of consciousness:

The Sixth Chakra: This is also known as the *frontal chakra or ajna* in Hindu terms. It can be found between the eyebrows or slightly above it, this is why it's also called as the 'third eye'. The ajna is known as the center of a person's psychic 'powers' because it can produce many psychic effects. When the ajna is couple with meditation, it can also help cure one's nervousness.

The Seventh Chakra: This is also known as the *crown chakra or sahasrara* in Hindu terms. It can be found at the top of a person's head or the pineal gland inside the brain. It is also referred to as the thousand petaled lotus, and it mostly relates to the astral/ emotional projection, and also enlightenment.

Tattvas System and Ceremonial Magic

Some occult groups also used the tattvas system (from Eastern culture) to refer to the magical elements. The symbols and colors used are very different from the systems in the western culture:

Magical Element	Tattva	Tattva Symbol
Earth	Prithivi	Yellow Square
Fire	Tejas	Red Triangle
Air	Vayu	Blue Circle
(spirit)	Akasa	Black Oval
Water	Apas	Silver Crescent

Techniques Used by Magicians

Yoga

One of the most common ways to enrich the mind, body, and spirit is through yoga. This technique is originally from India, but because of its many benefits to a person's lifestyle, it has now become widespread around the world. It is both a mental and physical discipline that conditions the body, invigorates the mind, and also attracts positive vibes or energies that improves one's life. You can use this technique to be able to connect deeply and strongly to your inner world and to the higher forms of energy from within you and the environment.

There are different kinds of yoga but it can be categorized into 3 types of yoga, these are the following:

- **Hatha Yoga:** Affects one's mind by training the body through different physical exercise. It can also help improve one's physical health, and promotes endurance.

- **Raja Yoga:** Affects one's mind by mental training. It mainly improves one's focus or concentration.

- **Mantra Yoga:** Affects one's mind by regular/ frequent affirmation or chanting. It also helps an individual to relax which can help if you're dealing with stressful events or environments.

Meditation

There are many techniques for meditation, and there are also many benefits to it just like the aforementioned benefits of yoga. Basically though, meditation has 2 main purpose or functions: to relax the mind, and to improve focus.

2 Main Functions of Meditation

- **Concentration Meditation** (improves focus)
  Most meditations can be classified under concentration meditation. This is where one focuses in one's attention in a single object/ physical material like a candle flame; in a sensation like focusing in one's breathing; in an emotion like love; in the mantra or chant being spoken either in one's mind/ aloud; or through visualization (chakra meditation). Simply put, concentration meditation is a form of self – hypnosis.

- **Insight Meditation** (improves Mindfulness/ Awareness/ Relaxation)
  This kind of meditation analyzes one's thoughts and feelings in a way where one can realize the subjectivity and also illusion of a person's experience. This can be done to attain transcendental awareness where one can sort of step out of the body or situation like when people say 'this body is not me.' Some examples include Buddhist meditation.

Mantras/ Chants

In terms of mantras or chants (involving words/phrases being repeated or chanted aloud), a powerful mantra that is commonly known is by using the mystical word "OM." This originated in Indian philosophy, as someone who intends to practice ceremonial magic; you can use this to turn universal vibrations in promoting feeling of positivity, peace, and also harmony. Most magicians use it to sort of prepare and get in the mood before doing any magic rituals as this technique can throw away 'negative forces, vibes or energies.'

What you can do to vibrate the mantra is to say it slowly yet aloud but in a low – pitched voice (lower than your normal speaking voice). Let the sound fade at the end of the chant. If you do this right, the 'OM' sound will seem to vibrate the energy around you. You can vocalize the word for about 10 seconds, and it should also be repeated many times for a few seconds. You can rest between vocalizations as it can sometimes cause dizziness especially if you're not used to doing it. Practicing it every day can surely make you feel connected to your inner world and touch the energies around you.

Chakra Meditation

Another technique you can do which is also under the category of concentrative meditation is called Chakra Meditation and is similar to Kundalini Yoga. This is the practice of causing one's psychic energy (kundalini) to flow the *sushumna* and energize the different major chakras. This type of meditation should be practiced with caution because it can be quite dangerous since it can produce physiological effects and sensations if it is applied for a long period of time. It's not advisable for those with mental – related problems or those with unstable mental conditions and even those with heart illnesses. This is because medications and drugs that are being used to treat such mental conditions can retard progress.

This technique is quite simple yet can definitely produce powerful and fast results. Some people report that results may appear right after hours of practicing it especially during sleep. It is also said that through this practice, each chakra in the body becomes energized and can also add sidhis or 'occult powers' until it reaches the crown chakra or the center found at the top of the head. Once this happens, enlightenment is achieved, though sometimes there'll be instances where the psychic energy/ kundaline can be awakened naturally.

When practicing Chakra Meditation, one should concentrate on the 7 major chakras, and must start with the root chakra (first chakra) before progressively moving up until the crown chakra thereby vivifying higher energies. Each chakra has its own certain qualities which mean that every time a person does this visualization technique, it can possibly raise one's consciousness, and also promotes astral projection. You can do Chakra meditation for at least 15 to 30 minutes a day. It can also be enhanced if you do hatha yoga or other physical exercise to make the spinal cord more flexible. Diet is also important as it can affect or improve the whole process. This technique is quite similar to Tibetan Tummo Meditation. You'll know if you do it right once you experience or feel a sort of vibration, buzzing, light or heat in your body rising.

Diet and Health

How you treat your physical body will surely have an effect on your mind. If you wanted to have an alert mind in (ceremonial) magic, it's also important that you take care of your body. Make sure that you are as healthy as you can be because a healthy body means a healthy mind. You can do this by doing the basic things everyday like regularly doing exercises, eating the right foods, taking vitamins or supplements, and as much as possible not consuming things that can be bad for your health like drinking too much alcohol, eating junk foods, taking prohibited drugs, or smoking because this can certainly have a negative effect on your mental health.

The golden rule is to always take everything in moderation. Make sure that you're aware of what you consume and how much you take. Many occultists or magicians highly recommend going on a dietary change like cutting down sugar, processed foods, and even avoiding meat as much as possible. The physical, mental, and spiritual effect of the foods you take cannot be denied. Such effect is often described as heaviness food factors. You can see in the chart below some examples of the rank of different foods from light to heavy:

Light Foods	Lettuce; green veggies
-	Fruits
-	Wheat, Grains, Rice
-	Nuts, Beans, most legumes
-	Cheese, eggs, other dairy products
-	Fish, Seafood
-	Chicken, Turkey, Poultry meat
Heavy Foods	Beef, Pork, other red meats

As what you have seen in the chart, red meats are harder to digest, and therefore considered as the 'heaviest' food group. Generally, foods that are higher in protein are 'heavier' than foods that are not. This means that most animal products are heavier than vegetables or plant produce. Foods that are also rich in carbs (such as candies, starch, and bread) are also heavy. The weight of foods though is not directly related to the amount of calories.

Why do you need to know this? What's the relation of what you eat when you perform magic? This is because the lightness or heaviness of food will certainly affect your 'magical experience.' If you tend to eat lighter foods or less food, you'll increase your psychic energy or reception. If you tend to eat heavier foods or eat uncontrollably, you tend to bring down your energy level down to earth.

Of course being on a diet or doing a dietary change will take a significant amount of time before you can actually see the effect on both your physical health and mental health. It's not also recommended that you take extreme diet changes like excessive fasting or prolonged starvation because it can certainly lead to malnutrition, and being malnourished is obviously not healthy. Achieving a healthy body (one that can be measured by your height, weight, BMI, and other physical factors) is very important in magic.

Your healthy eating may temporarily produce an effect but you should just keep doing this until your body adapts the new diet change. Healthy foods and a healthy lifestyle can ultimately make a person have a healthy well – being. Always keep in mind that good health is equivalent to have a good mental quality or attitude which you can use when doing magic.

The Four – Fold Breath

When it comes to doing physical exercises, it's best that you first consult a physician before you do anything (when in doubt, don't overdo) because not every exercise routines are good for everyone. There's no one – size – fits – all as some people have underlying health conditions (like respiratory or heart problems), therefore like in diet, moderation is still advised.

One of the best physical exercises that don't actually involve doing physical routines is call the four – fold breath. In India, this is known as *pranayama* (controlled breathing), which is a type of hatha yoga. If you're doing a four – fold breath exercise, calisthenics, or anything related to hatha yoga, you might want to do it under a timer so that you can also measure your progress. Basically, the longer you do these breathing/ yoga exercises, the better.

Pranayama's main goal is to relax one's mind and body. One of the best techniques is the four – fold breath exercise. Check out the steps below:

- **Step #1:** Take 4 quick inhalations and 4 quick exhalations. Repeat it until your allotted time is all used up (usually 3 minutes or longer). It normally takes about 1 ½ seconds of 4 inhalations and exhalations, or a total of around 3 seconds for a complete cycle/ repetition.

- **Step #2:** Make sure that there's no strain when doing the four – fold breath exercise. It's best that you do it while seating back in a chair without carrying anything and with your eyes closed so you can focus on your breathing.

- **Step #3:** You can start with 1 minute a day in your first week of doing the four – fold breath technique. After which you can gradually increase it to 3 to 5 minutes a day.

It's important to note that you might get to experience slight dizziness especially when it's your first time to do this because the common effect of this technique is hyperventilation. Make sure that you have someone to aid you or also guide you (say a yoga instructor or exercise guru) so that you'll be able to do it properly. This shouldn't be done if you're doing heavy lifting/ exercises (it might cause you to pass out) or if the air is polluted.

Doing the four – fold breath technique or other similar pranayama exercises (such as hatha yoga, walking, callisthenic exercises, running/ jogging) before you perform ceremonial magic can help your body and your mind get into the mood because it will relax you and also release stress, tension, and other negative vibes out of your system which will enable you to get more in touch of your inner world and have access to higher energies.

Chapter Five: Divination and Spirits

There are different types of divination but the major ones are astrology, tarot, geomancy, the I Ching, and also clairvoyance which is a form of direct psychic means. Forms of divination are usually used when one is performing a magic ritual because it is how a magician can communicate with spiritual beings or entities. It's more than a mechanical system, and it also implies psychic receiving or interpretation. Since divination happens in the mind, this means that it can be affected and biased by one's mind. The divination process and its interpretations (ceremonial magic, tarot reading, astrology etc.) can also be altered by the attitude, fears, and emotions of the one's self.

Just like in any other fields, the use of magic or divination can alter one's life or the outcome but not always. Using such methods can show tendencies which can be helpful to an individual, though it's not supposed to be something that rules a person's life because nothing is absolute because we don't really know what the future holds, and it's always changing.

This chapter will talk about concepts related to ceremonial magic such as developing clairvoyance abilities, having knowledge about thoughtforms and spirits as well as visualization exercise that one should do to prepare before doing the actual ritual that'll be discussed in the next chapter. Developing a strong mental health, psychic abilities, and having thorough knowledge about anything related to ceremonial magic are all essential so that you can get your desired result.

How to Develop Clairvoyance

As the old saying goes, practice makes perfect. Even if nothing's perfect, practicing can help a person develop and improve abilities for one to become excellent and close to perfection. It's the same thing when trying to develop your psychic abilities. Most people think that it's not real, but we do have the ability to influence our life and the world around us if we only know how to do it. If you want to become a magician or someone who wanted to learn the art of ceremonial magic, one of the skills or abilities you need to enhance is your natural clairvoyance. As mentioned earlier, visualization is very essential when doing ceremonial magic, developing your clairvoyance ability is also a good exercise for visualization. Here are some steps on how to do it:

Step #1: Look at the environment around you then close your eyes, and see that same environment/ surrounding in your mind.

Step #2: Open your eyes and check how accurate you imagined it. The results will not always be perfect but if you keep doing this, you'll improve your imagination/ visualization skills.

Step #3: This time before you repeat the exercise, use your physical eyes and see everything as if you're a child. Try to see the vividness of the color, focus on the details and the same time the surrounding as a whole until it all takes a glow. Close your eyes again, and repeat step #1.Capture this glow once you close your eyes, and picture the surroundings in your mind.

Step #4: Keep doing this, and also try out visualizing things in a different surrounding like a room, a building, a city, nature, the other side of the world etc.

Step #5: Do this exercise at least several times a day if you can. You just have to get it partly right, of course the more accurate, the better because that's how you know your clairvoyant abilities are improving.

The Aura

The aura is the colored light or perhaps a glow that one can see in other people. Using your clairvoyant abilities, the aura is sometimes seen as multi – colored glow around a person with various color layers and different zones. There are lots of occultists that claims to see an aura very easily but under varied condition but it could also just be optical illusions because sometimes the sight qualities can trick a person into thinking that he/she sees something of which one cannot see; this is the quality of sight known as the after image. Try doing this; stare at solid bright colored objects for a few seconds. Intense colors like red, green and blue will do the trick. Then look away, and stare at a white surface, usually what you'll see is the phantom image of the bright colored object in its complementary colors (red objects will be seen as green; blue will be seen as orange etc.) If this bright object is placed in front of a light surface, you'll most likely see a fringe of complementary colors around such object after a few seconds. Such observations are normal, and are also used by some magic occult groups to aid in the visualization process – this technique is known as flashing colors. Don't be fooled though because this flashing colors or after image are not actually the 'aura.' Some people think it is, especially those psychic frauds. When a real psychic sees the aura of a person, he/she is able to determine the mood or the emotional state of a person, and not just see some flashing colors or after image.

There are different meanings that are attributed to the colors of an aura. The chart below is based on Theosophical materials. You might encounter other books or groups that attribute different meanings to the colors of aura, but the difference in the chart you'll see below is that it's more emotional in nature. This can be useful if you're planning to do healing or an artificial elemental / spiritual entity. It is believed that if you surround yourself with your desired color, you'll tend to produce a specific psychological effect or emotion as described in the chart. Such qualities of color are very useful during magic rituals.

Colors of the Aura

Main Colors	Meaning	Sub - Colors	Meaning
BLACK	malice	dark gray pale gray	depression fear
BROWN	materialism	muddy gray or dull rust	selfishness
RED	energy	bright red dirty red dull red rose	anger and force passion and sensuality selfish love unselfish love
ORANGE	pride	orange cloud bright orange	irritability noble indignation
YELLOW	intellect	yellow-green earthy yellow lemon	low intellect selfish thought high intellect

		bright gold	logical thinking
		bright red - yellow	spiritual thought
GREEN	empathy	Gray - green	Deceit; jealously
		greenish-brown	jealousy
		emerald green	unselfish resourcefulness
		foliage green	sympathy and empathy
		bright apple – green	strong vitality
		bright turquoise	deep sympathy and compassion
BLUE	devotion (religious feeling)	Gray – blue	fetishism
		Light blue	noble spiritual devotion

		dark blue	religious feeling
		bright lilac – blue	lofty religious idealism
VIOLET	Spiritual; psychic & spiritual faculty		
WHITE	Purity; protection		

Thoughtsforms and Spirits

When a person concentrates in his/her own thoughts, one can draw psychic energy. This is the so – called thoughtform. Usually once an individual breaks concentration, the energy also tends to dissipate though it's very possible to concentrate energy in this way so that one can purposely produce strong thoughtforms. These thoughtforms are the centers and so – called vortexes of one's psychic energy. It can even exist as temporary entities by themselves even if it is basically non – thinking and inanimate forces/ energies. Talking to such inanimate forces is as logical as talking to a table. If you think about it, thoughtforms are quite similar to spiritual entities like elementals, and ghosts. Such psychic entities are made up of psychic energy vortex which is like a localized field or a form of discontinuity of the one's physical world.

Psychic entities or elementals usually respond to certain magnetic fields (electrostatic) or other energy centers, this is the reason why it responds in doing any magic ritual. Today, electronic machines are used when dealing with such elementals. These entities especially if the energy they possess is quite strong can affect one's thought process. It's important to note that these thoughtforms, ghosts, and elementals are usually not smart. If these entities do display some form of intelligence, it's usually limited as they are known to be the "morons of the spirit world." An artificial elemental's behavior is repetitive, and mostly automatic, some even call them as astral robots. There are also some spirits and deities that are volitional and smart.

The Art of Attention

Wherever you focus your attention, your mind and thoughts will follow too. Whenever you direct your attention to a specific object, purpose, or place that is where you focus your mental energy.

A concrete example is when you're eating at a crowded restaurant, you see everyone minding their own business and talking at once so you can imagine how noisy it is. If you somewhat noticed a person in the room, and you focus your attention to him/her, all of a sudden that person drops his fork, and you hear it hit the floor. If you hadn't focused your attention to that person, would you have heard the sound of the fork if you hadn't see it or focus on it? It's only because you keep your attention which is why you were able to pick the event and associate the sound with it.

This goes to say, that wherever your mind or attention is pointed, the rest is nothing or just a noise background. Noise can also be deemed as some sort of negative energy, emotions, attitudes, and thoughts. This makes it quite harder to concentrate and direct one's attention to something. Keep in mind that your thoughts lead to the emotions or feelings, but it's important to note that your emotions are NOT you. These are merely reactions prompted by your mind based on your model/ experiences.

If you learn how to direct your attention/ mind to a specific emotion, say feeling positive or happy or depressed, it will likely caused you to feel and experience such emotions. You can learn how to change your emotions if you know how to control your attention. Don't get me wrong, it's not about denying what you feel, you should in fact feel whatever your emotions are at the moment but it's also important to not dwell on it too long especially if it's a negative or the depressive type, you can do this by learning the art of attention or simply learning to focus on other perhaps more positive emotions.

Visualization Exercise Tips

Doing visual exercises is very essential in ceremonial magic. Below are some visualization exercises that can help you further develop your mental/ psychic abilities:

Exercise #1: Close your eyes, and try to imagine a single digit number as clearly as you can. Then imagine a 2 – digit number, then 3 - digit. Hold this visualization for at least 2 minutes every day. Repeat this exercise with words, letters or phrases and visualize it using your 'inner eye.'

Exercise #2: You can visualize a brightly colored green spot that is somewhat circular. Hold this visualization for at least 2 minutes. Then try it with a different bright color.

Exercise #3: You can also try visualizing tattvic symbols with their proper colors, and in succession. Hold each one for at least 2 minutes until you can see it accurately.

Exercise #4: You can also use tarot cards. Try picking your favorite card/s, and then study it and all its details (remember that it's best you see it vividly and let the colors glow). Close your eyes, and visualize it and see the details vividly, hold the image for 2 minutes. Repeat the process for other cards you want.

Exercise #5: You can also do the visualization exercises mentioned above with your eyes open.

Chapter Six: Basic Rituals of Ceremonial Magic

The basic rituals are known as the heart of ceremonial magic because this is the process that magicians are using to achieve what they desire or the magical results one intends to have. A magical ritual is also the procedure/ ceremony that magicians do in order to change, influence or alter their surroundings. Rituals can both affect active and passive magic, though the change achieved is mostly subjective and only in the physical plane/ world. Results can sometimes be subtle as well.

This chapter will cover the significance of rituals, the basic parts of a ritual, and how one can use ceremonial magic in creating artificial elementals. We also provided some tips on how you can do a successful ritual and achieve your desired result through ceremonial magic.

Believe and You're Halfway There!

Ordinary people who don't have any idea about ceremonial magic or those who have not studied it may sometimes refer to the results as something coincidental even if the effects can be seen in realty. Keep in mind that magical goals should be taken seriously especially when applied during rituals or ceremonies.

The success of the rituals performed during ceremonial magic highly depends on one's belief, therefore the first and foremost ingredient is to believe the system itself, or believe that the rituals can bring about results. It is said that if you believe strongly in whatever your desired result is – that act of believing is already a magical ritual itself, and can truly help in achieving one's desire or goal. Most people mistake that complex rituals creates better results or makes one achieve it faster, but for the magic to be effective, what one really needs is proper mindset, knowledge of the basics, and a very strong belief. Several techniques like concentration, meditation, breathing, and imagination will all come into play just as we've mentioned in previous chapters. In the context of training your mind to believe in something or perhaps changes a certain belief, one needs to practice another mental technique called "creative visualization."

Creative Visualization

In creative visualization, if you want to 'magically' have something or achieve a certain desire, you should first picture, visualize, or imagine it clearly in your mind. The more detailed and specific, the better! Make sure to have a clear idea of what you truly want to achieve, and make it as real in your mind as possible. You should also picture yourself already having what you desire or already doing what you desire. Some people say, it's best to imagine the end result, don't focus on the 'how' or the process of how something will come about, just focus and picture what you want to have, and imagine it as if you already have it.

It's highly advised that you concentrate on this thought, and hold it for a few moments. Be intense about it, you can also hold your breath for a few seconds while doing creative visualizations. Make sure to feel the energy in your body, the passion of your certain desire or dream welling up inside you. Then release it! Release the energy of your desire in your mind and out to the universe. You have to really feel the energy while you're holding that thought in your head as you intensify it, then imagine that energy exploding out of your head into the macrocosm/ universe as if you're the source of its life (because in a way you truly are), feel the universe move and react to the force you just released (you can also do this as you simultaneously release your breath). And then the last step is to believe. Believe that your dream, purpose and desire have been accomplished already, that the universe/ macrocosm is at work, that it's a done deal. You can also say "it is done" or something similar after you release your breath, your desire, and your energy into the universe.

This is not just an exercise, I've tried doing creative visualizations and so far, I have already achieved in reality all of the things/ desires that I wanted back then. I had no idea how in the world that happened, but it did. And I think it's because I truly believed in my heart that the universe will bring it to completion no matter how "impossible" it may be. Of course, you still have to do your part, and set goals, and put it into action but by firmly believing that you deserve to have it creates vibrations in the macrocosm that could definitely bring about your desired result.

Always remember, you are a force, you're made up of energy, your mind is the most powerful tool in the universe as it can shape everything and affect everything around you. You just have to believe that it will, and trust that something bigger than yourself will help you achieve whatever you want in life. If you learn this concept, you can surely create successful magic rituals.

Basic Parts of a Magical Ritual

The creative visualization exercise as discussed above is already in itself part of the ritual. Although, the magic rituals is of course more 'formal.' Any full magic ritual always consists of these 3 basics: imaging, building, firing. Some rituals must be repeated every day especially if the desired outcome is quite big or perhaps difficult, or do it every day in order to strengthen one's belief in something. Below are the basic parts of a ceremonial magic ritual:

The Magic Circle

In formal magic rituals, magic circle is one of the most important aspects. Many ancient and medieval magicians considered magic circles essential because of its exactness. There have been many elaborate designs that were developed over the years often coupled with layers of various words and symbols. The most important thing though is to make sure that there's no break in the circle, and that it is completely intact.

When doing the ceremony or ritual, the magician and also the participants (if any) must stand inside the circle because it will serve as the safe space and protection from evil forces or unwanted negative energies. Magic rituals usually begin by banishing evil forces and keep them outside of the magic circle. Today, magicians make circles by drawing one in the floor using a chalk, rock salt, rope or paint. Keeping in one's circle is very important especially when dealing with aversive elementals or spirit entities. Creating a magic circle is also helpful to concentrate the energy needed for the ceremony, and direct it toward one's purpose. A magic circle keep the energy contained until the magician or participants release it out. Magic circles have been the traditional symbol that's being prepared before doing any ritual or ceremony.

Artificial Elementals

As previously mentioned, a magician can create artificial elementals or spiritual beings. It is mostly used for the following reasons:

- It functions as an invisible observer or watcher that can tell a magician what it sees
- It functions as a psychic guard
- It can be used when healing
- It can be helpful in other ways depending on how the magician wants to use it.

A magic figure named Ophiel calls artificial elementals as "familiar." Producing an artificial elemental is quite easy, but it's important that you should already assume that such act have already produced results even if you don't get to immediately observe or see them. It's also possible to produce this spiritual creatures or entities and not know it because the magician is not clairvoyant enough to see/ observe it. This is why it's important, as one of magic's general rules, to not ignore whatever force you already have set in motion. You may not directly see it but you can still feel it nevertheless so be very careful.

Note: Never use artificial elementals for aversive magic purposes as it can be nasty to get rid of. If ever you need to eliminate them, you should learn how to re – absorb it through using your will or you can also exorcise it.

How to Create an Artificial Elemental

Creating an artificial elemental for various magical purposes requires clairvoyant abilities, visualization skills, and knowledge of all the concepts previously mentioned in this book. Artificial elementals are thoughtforms that had been strengthened by one's emotion. You can refer to the Color of the Aura chart in the previous chapter because it can be useful in creating what color to make the elemental or entities based on your intended purpose. Usually, apple green is the color used for general magic purposes. Once you decide on the color, you can now decide a shape – do you want the elemental to resemble a particular being or perhaps an animal? This is where creative visualization comes in. Make sure to visualize the form or shape of your artificial elemental, its aura and color and imagine it glowing before you.

You can strengthen it by communicating with your elemental through mental telepathy or by talking to it. Keep in mind that your elemental is connected to you and your subconscious mind/ attitude which means that it won't do things that you think it can't do.

In ceremonial magic, the trick in achieving results is to believe and make an effort in it. Look at your artificial elemental as something that is a part of your personality which has been detached from you.

Invocation

Doing a formal ritual usually involves calling celestial beings (such as a god, goddess or a deity), spirits, and other forms of entities. This is known as invocation. In a sense, magic can be related to pagan religion and also witchcraft, though magic rituals or ceremonial magic don't need worship, it's merely a technique that can be used to achieve results. Keep in mind also that invocation of entities can create artificial elementals.

According to Crowley, there are 3 main kinds of invocation, these are the following:

- **Devotion to an entity** (ex: Bhakti yoga of the Hare Krishna sect; Faustian devil pact)
- **Ceremonial Invocation** (method / technique used in the medieval period)

- **Drama** (usually involves a group or more a lot of people like in Holy Eucharist/ Mass)

And because of the microcosm – macrocosm concept, once a magician invokes a god/s, they are usually invoking aspects of themselves. Jung refer to gods or celestial beings as primitive archetypes, which sort of make it sound like such spiritual entities are only illusions of the mind, but in the concept of microcosm – macrocosm, it certainly does not discredit these deities, gods or goddesses because it helps illustrate man's relationship to the cosmos/ universe.

Reminders When Doing Magic Rituals

- **Balance in ceremonial magic is very important.** Make sure to vary the entities that you invoke to also keep your personality in balance.

- **Rituals usually produce side – effects.** Sometimes the side – effects is along the lines of the desired result. If your goal is delayed or hasn't happened yet, you might get to see the side – effects first. And if ever the goal/ desired outcomes in not achieved (as it can happen), these side – effects may be pronounced. Here's a concrete example: If you use a magic ritual to hurry a shipment of your package, you might end up getting the wrong one (this is the side – effect). Another example is if you do a magic ritual to cause a certain person to call you up, the side – effect could be that other people may call you except the one you intend to talk to. Side – effects will not affect you or anyone unless of course that's what you truly want.

- **Keep in mind that any form of ceremonial magic follows the so – called 'law of results.'** This only means that if you want results, you should make an effort to do so. If your goals is big or quite impossible or really difficult to achieve it usually has greater resistance or magical inertia that one should overcome. If the ritual didn't produce your desired outcome, the reason of failure is usually within oneself. You should also sort out issues of self – doubt and mental contradictions as it may interfere when doing rituals or achieving goals because you're not really decided if you truly want something or not. If this happens, make sure to re – program your mind by doing visualizations, meditations, and other similar mental techniques. Magical results happen if one also works in the physical level, don't just expect things to happen by themselves. Effort and action is still essential.

- **Time displacement is ceremonial magic's peculiar quality.** Results of magic rituals are not instantaneous. There's usually a delay of around 12 hours depending on the difficulty of the goal/ desire, and how strong/ weak the ritual is performed. Slight delay is fine; just give it time to get used to the changes that are coming. There are also some cases wherein the effects have already appeared even before the magic ritual is done.

- **Keep in mind that magic rituals or any similar occultism is very dangerous for people who are mentally unstable or have mental conditions.** Make sure you do mental exercises, eat the right foods, strengthen your chakras (as previously mentioned), and use your religious background or other belief system for support.

Chapter Seven: Healing and Banishing Rituals

Spiritual and psychic healing is a potential that all humans have. There are just those who tends to be better at using them but as what previous chapters have shown, a person can tap into their 'psychic powers' and bring out their chakras / energy to achieve certain desires (in this case, heal someone) through practice. In ceremonial magic, every ritual or ceremony starts with banishing to get rid of the negative energies or vibrations, the second one is invoking (calling higher sources of energies in the macrocosm/ universe), and then there's healing rituals as well.

Healing other people is much easier than healing oneself. This chapter will give you an overview of how to perform banishing rituals and do healing.

Healing

Aside from direct healing (healing where a person is present), there's also the so – called 'absent healing' wherein healing happens even at a distance. In theory, psychic healing is where sickness is characterized by the imbalance of vital energy, though sometimes this is not directly the cause. Psychic healing is the process wherein the magician or the healer transfers his energy to the one who is ill in order to repair and balance out the person's energy. However, if the healer overdoes the healing process wherein he doesn't take precautionary measures to sort of disconnect himself, he may find himself ill because of energy drain, and because it is also somewhat connected to the sick subject being treated. The healer or the magician must be as healthy as possible (mind, body, spirit) otherwise the magician could unintentionally transfer whatever ill health he may have to his/her subject making the situation worse. Here are the basic techniques/ steps of psychic healing:

- Creative Visualization
- Prayer
- Ritual

When it comes to healing, mild sickness may only need a treatment or two as compared to serious or major illnesses which would need healing treatment for a certain period of time. It's also important to note that psychic healing is best combined with medical treatment. It shouldn't replace medicine, hospital treatment, and a physician since the physical world is also involved when one is ill.

Of all the 3 basic techniques, creative visualization as you now know is quite the easiest to apply. When using creative visualization, the magician should first start by imagining that the person who's ill is getting better or completely healthy. It's also advised to use different colors found in the aura chart that would help in the psychic healing process (you can try bright apple – green, white, or rose pink). This method can also be combined with yoga wherein one can feel the energy from the solar plexus chakra. When doing absent healing, it's best to arrange a time or schedule of the treatment beforehand. You can do this by asking your subject to sit back while his/her eyes are close, and just be in a receptive state of consciousness.

The Banishing Ritual

One of ceremonial magic's most basic and useful rituals is the banishing ritual; it is also referred to as the lesser banishing ritual of the pentagram. A pentagram which is also known as the pentacle in tarot reading is a 5 – upward pointed star symbol.

The main function of a banishing ritual is that it provides psychic protection to the magician and to the subject. It can also help in healing since this ritual can form a protective barrier against negative energies or malevolent forces. The psychic barrier that banishing rituals bring about can be created to let a desired force or constructive energy enters with the exclusion of unwanted forces. This is why this banishing ceremony is one of the first and most essential steps if you're going to perform any formal ceremonial magic.

The magician performing the banishing ritual must use a 'magical weapon' like a ceremonial want, knife or even one's index finger in order to draw the pentagram at the four directions or so – called cardinal points. You'll also need to chant the Hebrew names of God while doing this.

Below are the basic steps of the banishing ritual. Do take note that this can vary depending on what kind of magical system or philosophy you'll be using. This is sort of the general way of how one can do it:

Step #1: Hold your magical weapon while you are facing east. Then, straighten out your arms in front of you.

Step #2: You'll need to use the full sweep of your arm in order to draw the pentagram in the air.

Step #3: Make sure to do the following instructions by starting at the lower left while sweeping your weapon to the right as described below:

Start by sweeping your weapon at the following approximate clock points:

- o Start at 7:30 position
- o Point at the 12 o'clock position
- o Point at the 4:30 position
- o Point at the 10:30 position
- o Point at the 2:30 position
- o Go back at the 7:30 position

While you are doing this make sure that your arm aren't bent at the wrist and elbow.

Step #4: While you are swaying your magical weapon at the points described above, you'll have to visualize the lines it creates forming a white vibrant start floating before you. You need to project energy for you to do this to achieve a floating five – pointed start that's gleaming. Visualize all of this as vividly as possible.

Step #5: The next step is to energize the star further through piercing its center using your magical weapon while saying these words: "Yod – He – Vau – He" in a tone that's slightly lower than your normal voice.

Step #6: After doing this, you need to turn slowly to the next direction or cardinal point in sequence right after doing this ritual facing the east:

- o South: Chant "Adonai Tzaboath"
- o West: Chant "Eh – Ei – He"
- o North: Chant "Agla"

As you turn to the next cardinal point/ direction, your arms should still be extended in the same manner. Then visualize a white line connecting to that cardinal point. Trace a similar pentagram at the clock points as mentioned above, and repeat the procedure while chanting the appropriate words assigned to the particular cardinal point.

Step #7: After doing this, you should complete the white line that is drawn back to the center of the eastern side of the pentagram. It's also important to note that the cardinal points/ directions should be in a clockwise order because if not, the ritual will have a different function.

The result of the banishing ritual should be a huge bright white pentagram that is floating at the four directions/ cardinal points through the magician's visualization. It must be all tied together by a bright white line. Once this is done, the magician can now imagine the pentagrams moving towards your home or a space thereby giving a protection barrier to everything within it.

Another primary function of the banishing ritual is to ward off 'psychic attacks.' Psychic attack happens when another person or magician consciously or unconsciously tries to harm you or cause any illness, nightmares, negative or sad emotions, accidents and even force you to do something against your own will. However, such things don't often happen since most magicians are mostly pure – hearted people. Psychic attack s can affect a magician depending on how vulnerable one is. If the magician knows how to tap into his true will then he/she is safe since the true will or one's inner power is the greatest protection there is. It's important to note that banishing rituals are not harmful; one can even use it to get rid of negative aspects of oneself.

Chapter Eight: The Astral Projection

Astral projection is also known as Out of the Body Experience (OOBE) is one of the popular topics in occult literature. Astral projection is where one can travel, go to places, and see other worlds while the physical body is sleeping. Experiencing astral projection is pretty much like dreaming during your sleep (since dreams are most likely astral projections of the unconscious mind); this also means that it's not dangerous. However, astral projection is quite difficult for most because people tend to forget their dreams once they wake up. This means that successful astral projection requires effort and practice for one to develop and improve this ability.

This chapter will cover an overview about astral projection and its forms, how you can tap into it to improve your magic abilities, and also help you gain more control of your consciousness. We'll also provide some techniques you can use to improve your astral projection ability as learning this method requires inner mental clarity, and mind alertness.

Dreams and Astral Projection

It is believed that dreams are the door to the mind's subconscious; this means that it can be used for psychological purposes, precognition, and also spiritual insight. The content of one's dream is mostly influenced by external sensations, and sounds. It's also influenced by events that happened the previous day as well as your recent mood, and through suggestions. A person normally dreams 4 to 5 times every night with at least 2 hour intervals. The longest form of dreams happens in the morning.

Usually people can remember their dreams upon waking up, so if you want to recall it, it's best that you jot down everything you can remember as soon as you woke up. It doesn't have to be exactly right, just write down what you can remember, and don't let the idea/ thought vanish away forever, and then just add as many details as you can. The more you try to remember your dream, and put it into writing, the easier you'll recall it. This is important especially when practicing astral projection because you would want to remember as much details as you can once you travel with your mind.

Types of Astral Projection

Astral projection is divided into 3 types or categories; these are the following:

- Mental Projection
- Astral Projection
- Etheric Projection

Mental Projection

Mental projection is pretty much just clairvoyance (remote viewing).This is where imagination comes in. When you experience mental projection, you're simply an observer and not a participant which is why sometimes the images or experience is not vivid. Nevertheless, mental projection is very important because this is how you can experience the next level which is the astral projection.

Astral Projection

In astral projection, this is the part where a person is able to travel through solid objects, though sometimes one cannot act on it or move a certain object. It's important to note that astral and mental projections are not confined in the physical world. One can travel in different realms, and into other worlds even in other planets.

Etheric Projection

In theory, etheric projection is where part of one's physical body (etheric/ vital part) has been transferred with your mind's projection, though it could be difficult to determine which body part in particular. Etheric projections are very near the physical world. There have been some rare reports wherein the entire physical body had been to another place as in teleportation. Another rare case is when the entire physical body exists and also acts in 2 separate locations at the same time, this is known as bilocation.

States of Consciousness

Scientists over the years have studied the brain's electrical activity using equipment like Electroencephalograph (EEG) wherein electrodes are being picked up from the brain, then goes through filtration and amplification in the machine which drives a graph recorder. This led to the discovering of a human's brain activity; it has many ranges or so – called 'states of consciousness,' these are the following:

- **Delta:** Deep sleep; trance state
- **Theta:** Day dreaming; memory
- **Alpha:** Tranquility; meditation; heightened awareness
- **Beta:** tension; normal consciousness

Based from the state of consciousness above, physical relaxation is mostly implied in the delta, alpha, and theta consciousness. One can reach these states through self – hypnosis, relaxation methods, and deep breathing. The threshold between our sleep and waking consciousness is called hypnogogic state (drowsy condition); this is where astral projection usually occurs or at least a part of it. If a person can control and be at the moment during the hypnogogic state, then Out of the Body Experience (OOBE)/ astral projection is possible.

Basic Techniques for Astral Projection

There are many techniques a magician can do in order to improve astral projection. Such techniques are mostly methods of mental conditions. Some form of altered consciousness is involved since no one can do it while fully conscious or awake. Here are the main techniques that are used to experience astral projection:

Technique#1: Dietary Practices

The practice of fasting, being a vegetarian, and eating light types of foods as what we've discussed in previous chapters. Foods like carrots and raw eggs can be beneficial as well. It's important to note that you shouldn't consume any food before doing astral projection (OOBE). If you're going to try it before you sleep, then do it 2 to 4 hours after you ate your food.

Technique#2: Muscular Relaxation

This is something used in self – hypnosis and hypnosis. If your body is physically relaxed, it can definitely assist in achieving that trance state. It usually begins by relaxing the toes, followed by muscles, and eventually throughout the entire body.

Technique#3: Yoga and Breath Techniques

Doing yoga exercises and different breathing techniques (like four – fold breath) are quite similar with physical/ muscular relaxation. Kundalini yoga is very relevant in astral projection because it's mostly concerned with altering consciousness.

Technique#4: Visualization Techniques

Visualization is very helpful because it can improve one's ability to picture a remote environment, and because it is also concerned with clairvoyance. Although visualization is mostly a practice of mental projection, it can go to the next level which is astral projection like what we've mentioned earlier. Here's how to do it:

- o Step #1: Picture a closed door on a blank wall
- o Step #2: Visualize a meditation symbol in the door

- o Step #3: Imagine that door opening, and you entering it.

Technique#5: Guided Imagery

Quite similar to visualization, only this time there's a guide from someone or someone is describing the remote place (such as guided meditation tapes/ podcasts)

Technique#6: Body of Light

This is from an old Golden Dawn method, wherein a person imagines a mirror image of themselves, and then gradually transferring one's consciousness/ sensation to the duplicate image of oneself – the so- called 'body of light.'

Technique#7: Strong Willing

Quite similar to creative visualization technique wherein one imagines experiencing a desire/ outcome as if it's happened. The only difference is that this method is when a person expresses one's strong desire through willpower while visualizing themselves doing it.

Technique#8: Dream Control and Dream Expansion

This is one of the best techniques you can do to further experience astral projection. Dream control is when a person becomes aware that he/she is in his/her dream while dreaming! You can do this by finding discrepancies in the dream like if you're flying or riding a horse and going in faraway places, or anything that you know you cannot otherwise do in reality. Once you've found these discrepancies while dreaming, you'll soon be aware that you're inside your dream, and you can be in control of your astral projection; you can then go in places/ realms/ worlds and do whatever you want. Dream expansion is simply a variation of your dream control. It's possible to extend a dream even after you've woke up by extending it, and directing your dream.

These techniques are quite simple, and tend to be the same with other methods discussed in this book, but it will require practice and effort. It's also important to note that the astral world is known as the "ghostland" into which a person passes after death which is why it's quite possible to see a dead person, elementals, ghosts, and other spiritual beings. Magicians are usually comfortable once they go into the astral world. The astral world is something that is also subjective to the magician's thoughts. Basically one's true will control the movements found in the astral realm, and many magicians believe that they also experience heightened 'magical ability' whenever they are in the astral world.

Chapter Nine: Cabala: The Art of Western Magic

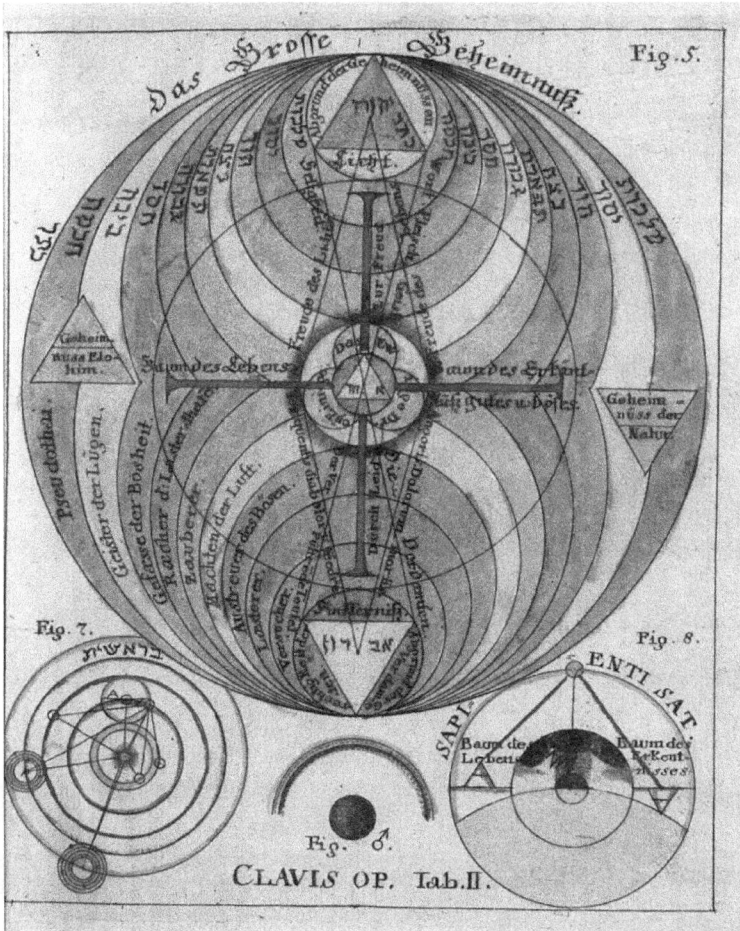

CLAVIS OP. Tab.II.

Cabala is a mystical tradition of the Jews that was first documented in the 12th and 13th century in France and Spain. Cabala is the basis of western ceremonial magic. Before being written down, the ceremony was orally passed on from generations possibly dating back to the time of the

Ancient Egyptians. This chapter will cover a bit of history about Cabala, the symbols involved and the attribution of each. You'll get a bit of history of how ceremonial magic and western magic came about.

Cabalistic Philosophy

In Cabala, the most important book is The Book of Creation, anciently known as Sephir Yetzirah, and the Book of Splendor also called as Zohar. Cabalistic philosophy is believed to have classified all of existence. There are four worlds in Cabala that is written in Hebrew and each of it has its own attributions, see the chart below:

Hebrew Name	Meaning of the Hebrew Name	Equivalent Worlds	Qualities
Atziluth	Archetypal World	Spiritual World	Pure deity
Briah	Creative World	Mental World	Archangels
Yetzirah	Formative World	Astral World	Angels
Assiah	Material World	Physical World	Action

In Cabala, the divine name of God is called Tetragrammaton. It is based from Hebrew letters Yod (English letter equivalent Y) He (English letter equivalent H) Vau (English letter equivalent V) He (English letter equivalent H). The Hebrew letter YOD corresponds to the element of fire and Atziluth; the first Hebrew letter HE corresponds to the element of water and Briah. The first two Hebrew letters is the yang – yin pair respectively, though the last two also forms the same yang – yin pair; VAU corresponds to the element of air and Yetzirah; the second HE corresponds to the element of earth and Assiah.

When it comes to the Cabalistic parts of the soul, it uses new terms for the 3 highest vehicles of consciousness:

- o Neshamah (Divine soul): Spiritual Body
- o Ruah (Moral soul): Mental Body
- o Nefesh (Animal soul): Astral Body

Sefirotic Tree (Otz Chieem)

The Sefirotic Tree is also known as the Tree of Life, and it is the most important attribute in Cabala philosophy. The Tree of Life represents the universe. It states that the universe consists of 10 sefiroth (this is the orders of creation) that is drawn as circles and in a descending pattern starting from the highest aspect of God (from the top) to the physical aspect of the world (bottom). The diagram below is the Serfirotic Tree wherein the sefiroth are linked through paths (numbered lines). Refer to Cabala books for better diagram version as several paths are omitted.

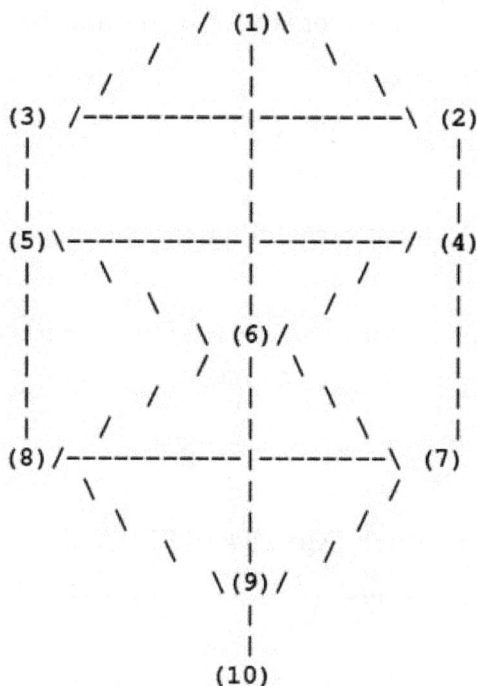

```
                    /  (1) \
                  /     |     \
                /       |       \
       (3) /----------|----------\ (2)
          |            |            |
          |            |            |
          |            |            |
       (5) \-----------|----------/ (4)
          |    \       |      /     |
          |      \     |    /       |
          |        \ (6) /          |
          |        / |  \           |
          |      /   |    \         |
          |    /     |      \       |
       (8) /---------|--------\ (7)
              \      |      /
                \    |    /
                  \  |  /
                  \ (9) /
                     |
                     |
                   (10)
```

The top of the Tree of Life is called the infinite void – this is the un - manifested God or the unknowable. There are also the 3 veils of negative existence, these are the following:

- Ain
- Ain Sof

- Ain Sof Aur

The Divine Light or also known as Ain Sof Aur is manifested by the 1st sefira where it is transformed into a more positive existence. The magical current or emanations of energy flow from the 1st sefira (or the source) along the paths into other sefiroth which also transform to lower levels of sefiroth. The process of creation is one of the emanations from the spiritual to the physical (from the top of the Tree of Life down to the Sink/ bottom). All current of the energy is sourced from the Tree of Life must be sinked to the earth. In ceremonial magic, magical energy that is set in motion through rituals should be used up in the physical realm whether or not the ceremony was a success.

The Supernal Triangle consists of Sefiroth 1, 2, 3 is something that is beyond the human experience in Atziluth's world. Kether is the first sefira which is also known as the supreme crown of God, and it signifies as the Source and pure being. Kether is also androgynous. Immediately rising from Kether are 2 emanations. The second sefira is known as Hokmah, this is also known as God's wisdom and the masculine force of the macrocosm. The third sefira is called Binah, which represents the intelligence of God, also known as the supernal mother.

The Abyss is something that is between these supernals and the rest of the sefiroth. This is the space in which forever separates the ideal from reality. The abyss is also where the 11th sefira called Daath is, where the God's knowledge is sometimes placed.

The world of Briah consist the 4th, 5th, and 6th sefiroth in the 2nd triangle. This is also known as the Mental Triangle. Hesed is the 4th sefira which is God's love and mery, and is also male and positive. Gevurah is the 5th sefira which is known as the power of God or God's strength wherein it complements Hesed as justice. The 6th sefira is known as Tifareth also known as God's beuty or compassion, and is the heart of the macrocosm/ universe.

The Astral Triangle (the third triangle) is composed of sefiroths 7, 8, and 9 in Yetzirah. The 7th sefira is called Netsah which is God's everlasting endurance and victory. Hod is the 8th sefira which also complements Netsah. It is known as God's splendor and majesty. Yesod is the 9th sefira and is the foundation of the world, it is also links with the moon hence the tides. Yesod is quite important in magic and astral projections. It is also usually experience as dream consciousness.

In terms of the physical realm of Assiah, the 10th sefira is Malkuth which is God's kingdom. It is also the basis of all physical creation. People experience it as sense consciousness.

The Sefirotic Tree also has 3 pillars. The pillar on the right as you face the tree is headed by Hokmah, and ending with Netsah is known as the Pillar of Mercy. The Pillar of Mercy has yang (masculine) and light qualities. The pillar on the left headed by Binah and ending with Hod is called the Pillar of Severity which has yin (female) and dark qualities. The one between them that equilibrates or balances the two opposites is known as the Middle Pillar, this is known as the Shekhinah (God's feminine counterpart). There are also evil demons known as Klippoth because in Assiah's world or the physical world it represents excesses or unbalanced forces.

All the universe's qualities fits like a puzzle in the Sefirotic Tree, each paths is a numeric key to various correspondence tables. Each sefira or parts has its own colors. The paths between the sefiroth also have their own colors and attributes. There are 4 color scales in the tree, and each one corresponds with one of the four worlds. This means that there's a separate sefirotic tree for each world. Briah (Queen) and Atziluth (King) scales are the most important. The table below shows the Briah and Atziluth scales:

Key	King Scale (Atziluth)	Queen Scale (Briah)
1	brilliance	pure white brilliance
2	pure soft blue	gray
3	crimson	black
4	deep violet	blue
5	orange	scarlet red
6	clear pink rose	yellow (gold)
7	amber	emerald green
8	violet purple	orange
9	indigo	violet
10	yellow	citrine, olive, russet, black

There are 22 paths that link the sefiroth together. The 22 paths also correspond to the Hebrew letters that is based in the Sefir Yetzirah book (Book of Creation). The Book of Creation divides each of the 2 letters in 2 dual parts. The chart below also shows the corresponding colors and location of the numeric paths in relation to the sefiroth. This is pretty much just the continuation of the table above.

Key	Joins Sefiroth Path	King Scale (Atziluth)	Queen Scale (Briah)
11	1 - 2	Bright pale yellow	sky blue
12	1 - 3	yellow	purple
13	1 - 6	blue	silver
14	2 - 3	emerald green	sky blue
15	2 - 6	scarlet	red
16	2 - 4	red orange	deep indigo
17	3 - 6	orange	pale mauve
18	3 - 5	Amber	Maroon
19	4 - 5	greenish yellow	deep purple
20	4 - 6	yellowish green	slate gray
21	4 - 7	violet	blue
22	5 - 6	emerald green	blue
23	5 - 8	deep blue	sea green

24	6 - 7	green blue	dull brown
25	6 - 9	blue	yellow
26	6 - 8	indigo	black
27	7 - 8	scarlet	red
28	7 - 9	violet	sky blue
29	7 - 10	crimson (ultra - silver white violet)	buff, flecked
30	8 - 9	orange	gold yellow
31	8 - 10	glowing orange scarlet	vermilion
32	9 - 10	indigo	black
31b	-	white merging nearly black into gray	deep purple
32b	-	citrine, olive, russet, black	amber

Both the King and Queen scales are complementary, just like the paths and sefiroth. Traditionally, the use of the king scale sefiroth will find the queen scale and vice – versa. The use of the complementary scales is usally based on the magician's idea of balance. Usually in most ceremonial magic, a tree composed of sefiroth which is in the queen scale; and the paths which are in the king scale is all you need.

The Tree of Life in ceremonial magic serves as the map of consciousness is very useful when understanding and achieving various states of consciousness. The main concern in cabal magic or cabalistic philosophy is the connection of the higher energies to the lower levels on the tree. It is a subject in itself is cabal path work (way of return) wherein one attempts to climb up the ladder of lights (tree) in order to attain union with the divine.

Chapter Ten: Psychic Energy

Based on the theories of magic, we now realized that there's definitely that the 'outer world' is linked and connected to the inner worlds as in the microcosm / macrocosm theories. You have also seen this in the four worlds; the philosophy of Cabala, and Tree of Life as well as the theory of correspondences which only means that the inner and outer world's relationship is very essential when performing ceremonial magic. It can also imply that because of this relationship, success or the lack thereof in either the inner or outer world influences and reflects the success or lack thereof in either worlds. This means to say that it's not enough for a magician to just learn how to meditate, rely on magical abilities, or does a surface – level practice; it implies that a magician should be excellent and become a master of the 4 worlds. Keep in mind that a real magician is one who is not just the master of the inner worlds but also of himself. It's also important to note that proficient magicians are all 'perfect,' but they have this positive personality that enables them to fully control their inner world and also influence the outer world. In the Book of Law, magicians are usually described as "Kings," this is because they are balanced in all aspects of life, and they can do whatever they want, and be who they want to be.

This chapter will cover other important topics that precede the lessons in the Cabala philosophy, the importance of psychic energy in magic, and how to use willpower in order to improve one's magical abilities.

Planetary Correspondences

The table below shows the key numbers that precedes the lessons you've learn in the Cabala philosophy chapter. These key numbers can also be found in different correspondence tables. You can use the table below for starters; this is one of the important set of correspondence for the planets are found below; the metals which are associated with the planet and the qualities of each is also included:

Key Numbers	Planet	Metal	Qualities
3	Saturn	lead	home
4	Jupiter	tin	Luck; wealth
5	Mars	iron	Anger; war-like
6	Sun	gold	vitality
7	Venus	copper	love
8	Mercury	mercury	knowledge

9	Moon	silver	Emotions; travel

In Cabalistic magic or Cabala theory, one should select the necessary planet in order to achieve a certain result. You can select the appropriate one through looking at the qualities or its attributes. When a planet is selected, an entity is can be matched by matching the key number using the correspondence table. Some tables may also show various deities and its corresponding attributes from different popular pantheons.

Hebrew Mysticism is where Cabala philosophy originated though it is mostly unconcerned with the magical implications of the philosophy. The question is, how can a monotheistic religions philosophy like Hebrew Mysticism gave credibility to a polytheistic kind of approach? It is because different deities are understood with having characteristic or attribute of the Supreme God but it's not a contradiction, just a restatement of the concept of the microcosm/ macrocosm relationship again. As what you now know, the Sefirotic Tree (Tree of Life) represents the whole universe or otherwise known as macrocosm. And even if one could say that each sefiroth has its own separate attributes, it is still part of the whole Tree of Life, and of the universe. This is why the pantheon belief system is very compatible and aligned with Cabalistic ideas.

Willpower and Magic

The Western magic philosophy traditionally emphasizes a great deal when utilizing one's willpower in order to develop one's magical abilities, and also improve on self – mastery. However, this may not be the best way in the long term. According to Isaac Bonewitz, a person's subconscious can sometimes go against the willpower with unwanted results which is why according to him, it's much better to control one's life democratically.

In Hawaiian Kahuna ceremonial magic, it talks about the 3 selves; the subconscious or lower self, the normal consciousness of a person or the middle self, and the spirit/ holy guardian angel or the high self. In the Hawaiian Kahuna system, for one to be enlightened means that the 3 selves should be unified and even become close to each other as much as possible. This is because according to this system, enlightenment comes from great acceptance, and not from great or sudden change. It challenges the notion that continual improvement at becoming better takes a man nowhere, because becoming it, is not being it. Unifying the 3 selves can be attained by first and foremost developing the communication with the inner world (subconscious) and the higher self. You can do this by doing simple and various mental/ spiritual exercises like automatic writing, self – hypnosis, raised finger responses, dream analysis, pendulum, and other things like meditation/ visualization. These exercises can facilitate communication with one's subconscious. It is also possible to later communicate with one's higher self after mastering communication via the subconscious, once this happens it means that there's a degree of unification of your three selves.

Psychic Energy

Many occult magic groups follow a particular energy theory for the ceremony and the physical body. This is equivalent to the psychic energy with prana, kundalinin or life force energy. The purpose of kundalini yoga is to raise the energy to the body's higher chakras in order to further enhance one's psychic powers or magic abilities. The releasing of this psychic energy/ powers is also relevant and beneficial to one's mind, health, and vitality as well as the achievement of tapping into the cosmic consciousness. Meditation and doing yoga is mostly used to free one's psychic energy so that it can be used when doing ceremonial magic or magic rituals, but aside from doing kundalini yoga and other types of meditation there are other ways to free up this psychic energy.

The techniques you'll see below functions as mental catharsis because it will in a way invigorate one's psyche which can result to improved intellectual and body performance.

- Different Types of Psychotherapy: Psychotherapy can releases pent up psychic energy.

- Mind games, inhibition, and other forms of extreme risks: These activities are also the basis of different mind practices. Some psychotropic drugs can also create these effects, and can give kicks from extreme risks like doing skydiving.

- Vigorous dances and physical exercises

- Various religious practices, and rituals

- The way of return and other sort of mystical practices

- Atavistic Resurgence: This is Austin Spare's technique wherein one is in contact with their primitive emotions that is buried deep within their psyche. It is quite regressive in some way but there's certainly power there if a person can learn how to control it.

Conclusion

Now you have seen how ceremonial magic and its theories/ philosophies is mostly based on the assumption that psychic phenomena is real because if this is the case then that means that magic is very real. Many people have seen how the systems of magic is somewhat the art and science of causing change that is in accordance with one's will through non – physical means. Needless to say, magical philosophy is the working system of symbols, rituals, theories, and terms but it also goes beyond that. It is an ancient system of psychology for our ancestors, and a method to improve oneself, and a system that can make a person's mind and spirit grow. Ceremonial magic and mysticism are considered as parallel paths both leading to transcendence.

Photo Credits

Page 1 Photo by user cocoparisienne via Pixabay.com,

https://pixabay.com/en/human-girl-child-face-fee-magic-3056693/

Page 2 Photo by user cocoparisienne via Pixabay.com,

https://pixabay.com/en/woman-fee-moon-star-astronomy-3084129/

Page 8 Photo by user shapkasushami via Pixabay.com,

https://pixabay.com/en/divination-background-krupnyj-plan-3101237/

Page 19 Photo by user kellepics via Pixabay.com,

https://pixabay.com/en/fantasy-landscape-cave-sun-light-2945514/

Page 26 Photo by user Activedia via Pixabay.com,

https://pixabay.com/en/meditation-spiritual-yoga-1384758/

Page 42 Photo by user JanBaby via Pixabay.com,

https://pixabay.com/en/ascension-celestial-planet-heaven-1568162/

Page 55 Photo by user RobertCheaib via Pixabay.com,

https://pixabay.com/en/candle-prayer-religion-faith-1912947/

Page 67 Photo by user Kellepics via Pixabay.com,

https://pixabay.com/en/fantasy-human-structure-mysticism-2964231/

Page 75 Photo by user Kellepics via Pixabay.com,

https://pixabay.com/en/fantasy-landscape-monument-child-3097474/

Page 85 Photo by user Cesar Ojeda via Flickr.com,

https://www.flickr.com/photos/odisea2008/13922060825/

Page 97 Photo by user Eddi van W. via Flickr.com,

https://www.flickr.com/photos/spiritual_marketplace/3203729256/

References

A Definition of High, or Ceremonial, Magic –

Thoughtco.com

https://www.thoughtco.com/ceremonial-magic-p3-95830

Astral Projection – Wikipedia.org

https://en.wikipedia.org/wiki/Astral_projection

Beginner's Guide to the 7 Chakras – AboutMeditation.com

http://aboutmeditation.com/beginners-guide-chakras/

Cabala – Wikipedia.org

https://en.wikipedia.org/wiki/Cabala

Ceremonial Magic – Wikipedia.org

https://en.wikipedia.org/wiki/Ceremonial_magic

Ceremonial Magic – WorldSpirituality.org

http://www.worldspirituality.org/ceremonial-magic.html

Ceremonial Magic and Sorcery – Sacred – texts.com

http://www.sacred-texts.com/eso/sta/sta24.htm

Chakra Meditation: Balancing Your 7 Chakras – MindBodyGreen.com

https://www.mindbodygreen.com/articles/how-to-balance-the-chakras-with-meditation

Is Astral Projection Real? – World – of – Lucid – Dreaming.com

http://www.world-of-lucid-dreaming.com/astral-projection.html

Mastery of the elements – White Magic Love

https://www.white-magic-love-spells.info/mastery_of_the_elements.html

Parapsychology – Wikipedia.org

https://en.wikipedia.org/wiki/Parapsychology

Tree of Life: Magical Formulae - Thelemapedia.org

http://www.thelemapedia.org/index.php/Tree_of_Life:Magical_Formulae

Tree of Life: Magical Powers - Thelemapedia.org

http://www.thelemapedia.org/index.php/Tree_of_Life:Magical_Powers

Tree of Life: The Quarters - Thelemapedia.org
http://www.thelemapedia.org/index.php/Tree_of_Life:The_Quarters

Tree of Life: Magical Weapons - Thelemapedia.org

http://www.thelemapedia.org/index.php/Tree_of_Life:Magical_Weapons

The Four Worlds – Digital – Brilliance.com

http://www.digital-brilliance.com/themes/fourworlds.php

The Differences between the 5 Major Types of Magic – Thoughtco.com

https://www.thoughtco.com/types-of-magic-95961

The Tree of Life: The Four Worlds - Thelemapedia.org

http://www.thelemapedia.org/index.php/Tree_of_Life:The_Four_Worlds

Types of Magic – Hidden Legacy

http://hiddenlegacy.ilona-andrews.com/types-of-magic/

You are a Microcosm of the Macrocosm – The Master
Shift.com

https://themastershift.com/you-are-a-microcosm-of-the-
macrocosm/

Introduction to Ceremonial Magic – Sacred – Magick.com

http://www.sacred-
magick.com/Articles/Introduction%20to%20Ceremonial%20
Magick/Introduction%20to%20Ceremonial%20Magick.pdf

Feeding Baby
Cynthia Cherry
978-1941070000

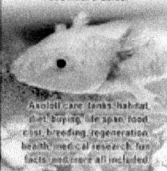

Axolotl
Lolly Brown
978-0989658430

Dysautonomia, POTS
Syndrome
Frederick Earlstein
978-0989658485

Degenerative Disc
Disease Explained
Frederick Earlstein
978-0989658485

Sinusitis, Hay Fever,
Allergic Rhinitis Explained
Frederick Earlstein
978-1941070024

Wicca
Riley Star
978-1941070130

Zombie Apocalypse
Rex Cutty
978-1941070154

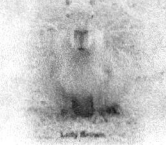

Capybara
Lolly Brown
978-1941070062

Eels As Pets
Lolly Brown
978-1941070167

Scabies and Lice Explained
Frederick Earlstein
978-1941070017

Saltwater Fish As Pets
Lolly Brown
978-0989658461

Torticollis Explained
Frederick Earlstein
978-1941070055

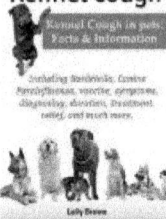

Kennel Cough
Lolly Brown
978-0989658409

Physiotherapist, Physical
Therapist
Christopher Wright
978-0989658492

Rats, Mice, and Dormice
As Pets
Lolly Brown
978-1941070079

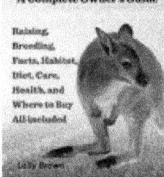

Wallaby and Wallaroo Care
Lolly Brown
978-1941070031

Bodybuilding Supplements
Explained
Jon Shelton
978-1941070239

Demonology
Riley Star
978-19401070314

Pigeon Racing
Lolly Brown
978-1941070307

Dwarf Hamster
Lolly Brown
978-1941070390

Cryptozoology
Rex Cutty
978-1941070406

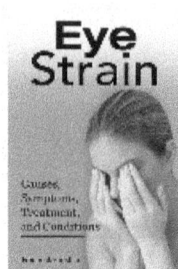

Eye Strain
Frederick Earlstein
978-1941070369

Inez The Miniature Elephant
Asher Ray
978-1941070353

Vampire Apocalypse
Rex Cutty
978-1941070321

www.ingramcontent.com/pod-product-compliance
Lightning Source LLC
Chambersburg PA
CBHW052113090426
42741CB00009B/1794